THE FIRST BOOK OF
COMMON-SENSE
MANAGEMENT

THE FIRST BOOK OF
COMMON-SENSE
MANAGEMENT

How to Overcome Managerial Madness by Finding the Simple Key to Success

Diane Tracy

William Morrow and Company, Inc.
New York

MONTROSE LIBRARY DISTRICT
434 SOUTH FIRST STREET
MONTROSE, COLORADO 81401

67595

Copyright © 1989 by Diane Tracy

All rights reserved. No part of this book may be reproduced or utilized in any form or by any means, electronic or mechanical, including photocopying, recording or by any information storage and retrieval system, without permission in writing from the Publisher. Inquiries should be addressed to Permissions Department, William Morrow and Company, Inc., 105 Madison Ave., New York, N.Y. 10016.

Library of Congress Cataloging-in-Publication Data

Tracy, Diane.
The first book of common-sense management / Diane Tracy.
p. cm.
ISBN 0-688-08346-3
1. Supervision of employees. 2. Supervisors. I. Title.
II. Title: First book of common-sense management
HF5549.12.T73 1989
658.3′02—dc 19   88-22835
                                                                                          CIP

Printed in the United States of America

First Edition

1 2 3 4 5 6 7 8 9 10

BOOK DESIGN BY NICOLA MAZZELLA

Acknowledgments

My sincere thanks to the mentors in my life who have shown me that compassion and common sense are the keys to being an effective manager. Thanks to Richard Koff for his expert help in editing my work.

Contents

Introduction

This book is a common-sense guide to management. It is based on the simple premise that in order to meet the objectives of the company, management must meet the needs of employees.

If good management consists merely of common sense and humanity, why is it so uncommon in the business world today? The truth is that fear often rules in the workplace. Managers are in constant terror of losing their power. In fact, managers are afraid to even *seem* to be losing their power, because in the business world the appearance of power *is* power.

When fear rules relationships, there is bound to be misunderstanding, distrust, hidden agendas. Common sense goes out the window. The result is that people suffer and productivity plummets.

When people are constantly on guard, politicking for power or protecting themselves, they have little time for building products and delivering services.

Are managers so blind that they cannot see how their behavior affects the people who report to them? The answer is yes—they are too busy protecting their own vulnerabilities.

Politics, of course, will always be present in the workplace to some degree, but there are things management can do to minimize the game playing that is so destructive. For starters, managers can apply the principles described in this book.

The way people within a company manage is reflected in the corporate culture of the organization, and corporate cultures are difficult to change. It is true that good management starts at the top and inexorably seeps down to lower levels, but even the best new company president isn't going to be able to overcome years of habit in a day or in a hundred days. Old patterns die hard, they don't just fade away.

But corporate cultures can be changed and it doesn't have to start in the boardroom. Each manager is at the top of a pyramid that extends downward. His influence is felt by the managers who report to him and the managers who report to them—all the way down the line to the lowest-level employee.

Regardless of where you may be working within the organization, you can make a difference. If you are an experienced manager, the principles outlined in this book will serve as a good reminder to you. If you are new to the position, the application of these principles will get you off on the right foot and put you on the road to success as a manager.

CHAPTER 1.

But What Does a Manager Do?

This morning your promotion finally came through. You have a title that includes words like *group leader, supervisor, director, manager.*

Clearly it was a promotion; you can tell because you now have

- more money—a little, anyway
- a larger desk or office
- a lot more responsibility

What you don't have is

- freedom to worry only about yourself
- overtime pay
- the right to forget about the job when you go home at night

Why Are Managers Usually Paid More Money?

And what does a manager do to earn it?

Easy answer:

- A plumber fixes pipes
- A carpenter cuts wood
- A bricklayer lays bricks
- A salesperson sells things
- An accountant counts things
- A manager manages people

It's *harder* to manage people than to fix pipes, cut wood, lay bricks, or count things because people are infinitely more complex.

What's Involved in Managing People?

To be a good manager you have to be a

- psychologist
- cheerleader
- friend
- teacher
- taskmaster
- leader
- listener

. . . and that's just for starters.

Your First Days on the Job . . .

During your first days on the job we suggest you apply the first principle of good management:

The Lay-Low Principle of Management

Certainly for the first few days, and maybe for a good long time after that—at least until you know what the heck is going on—

- Stay calm
- Listen to everything
- Say as little as possible

In short

Keep your eyes open
. . . and your mouth shut.

Be Warned!

It is very easy to make a mistake, particularly during those first few hectic days on the job, and then it may take weeks and maybe years to correct them.

There are ten cardinal rules of what <u>NOT</u> to do during the first few weeks as manager:

1. Don't Take an Ego Trip

Don't come on like John Wayne, sweep away all the old rules and procedures, tell everyone that "Things are going to be DIFFERENT now that I'm in charge."

Certainly some things are going to be different, but many others got the way they are for good reason. Until you know for sure why they are being done that way it makes sense to be very careful about changing them.

2. Don't Make Careless Promises

First, you can't buy friendship or loyalty.

Second, never promise anything you aren't absolutely certain you can deliver.

Third, rewards should be handed out very slowly, if at all, until you get your feet under you and you know exactly who is deserving of rewards.

Fourth, rewards should be handed out only for what people may have done in the past and what they are going to continue to do in the future.

3. Don't Play Genghis Khan

Oddly enough, acting like a tyrant is more likely to reveal your insecurities than your strengths. If you start ordering people around as if they were slaves you are going to create enemies you don't need. In the extreme you will start a revolution—which is hardly a convincing demonstration to *your* boss that you are a good leader.

Remember that true power is most often displayed in a quiet, firm manner that takes for granted orders will be followed. If *you* believe in your authority, so will everyone else.

4. Don't Play Favorites

One of the critical characteristics of a good leader is that he be fair in the treatment of subordinates. You know yourself that when you report to someone who praises or rewards only his cronies your morale drops, your interest in the job disappears, you get angry and frustrated. Why should you try to do your best if it will be ignored in favor of a teacher's pet?

It's a basic law of human nature—everyone thrives on praise and recognition. We like feeling special and important and if that is denied us we usually stop wasting our time or energy in thankless effort.

5. Don't Babble Without Thinking

With a ready audience hanging on your every word it is sometimes easy to forget that your staff is responding to your power over them, not necessarily your brilliance. It is easy to be seduced by all this attention, particularly if you are a little nervous in the beginning.

Next thing you know, you are babbling away. You can be sure that listeners are recording every stupid, thoughtless remark you make and that these remarks will probably come back to haunt you.

6. Don't Hoard the Work

The buzz word for this is *delegation*. Often out of nervousness or impatience, or simply because you don't trust subordinates to do the job right, you find yourself trying to do it all.

Pretty soon your desk is stacked with memos waiting for your approval. Decisions don't get made. Work gets backed up and your group or department becomes the company bottleneck.

This is by no means an unusual problem. Every manager who cares about the work feels an almost overwhelming sense of responsibility and it may seem easier and less time consuming to do it yourself than to show someone else how.

But training and delegation are among your most important responsibilities as a manager. Neglect them and you invite disaster.

67595

7. Don't Pass the Buck

The rule of good management is that when things go wrong in your area it's your fault; when things go right it's because of the people who report to you.

When a manager tries to shift the blame to employees he ends up losing their trust and respect.

Loyalty is a two-way street.

Remember, credit multiplies, blame divides.

8. Don't Throw Temper Tantrums

A sure sign of childish behavior is losing your temper, shouting, screaming, pounding the desk, throwing things, swearing. People don't see that as tough but simply crazy and untrustworthy. Pretty soon you'll be the last to hear the bad news, any bad news, and by the time you do it'll be too late to do anything about it.

It is your job to solve problems, not create them. This takes incredible patience and self-control. You don't have to deny your feelings. You wouldn't be human if you didn't get frustrated and angry at times. The trick is to be frustrated or angry at the *things* that are going wrong, *not the people,* even though they may be responsible.

9. Don't Take Special Privileges

As a manager you may suddenly have the opportunity to come in late, go home early, take long lunch hours, make a lot of personal calls. Impressed with your own importance, you may be tempted to exercise these symbols of your power.

But remember, you are on a stage and everyone is watching you. You are an example to the people who report to you and if you don't set the example they won't follow. You can't expect them to give you 100-percent effort if you're not around to see and appreciate it.

If you put in extra time, work extra hard to get the work out, the message will be clear as to what you value and will reward.

10. Don't Be Too Much of a Company Man or Too Much of a Buddy

It's a fine line you have to walk between loyalty to the company and loyalty to the people who report to you. If you lean too much toward the company because you see your own future there, your staff will see you as a toady. If you are too chummy with your staff you'll have difficulty maintaining authority.

Don't tell your people how you hate the company and plan to leave as soon as you get another job lined up. Don't share intimate details about last night's date.

It's unfortunate but true—the old buddy relationships can't be carried into the new situation. You're the boss now and you have to accept and use the distance that that implies.

How a Manager Spends His Time

We've spent a lot of time talking about what a manager is, and how he should behave. But what does a manager actually do all day?

His primary responsibility is to get the work done through other people. This may mean getting the products manufactured and off the production line, getting them packaged, shipped, or sold. It may mean providing customers with quality service and keeping them happy. It may mean getting the letters written or typed, getting the company purchases into the plant on time and at a good price.

Your boss doesn't care if you are going through midlife crisis, your bank account is overdrawn, or your kids have the measles. His main concern is that the job get done correctly and on time.

The next question is how does the manager do his job?

1. Keep Employees Safe

Efficiency may be a dirty word to some people but it has a simple meaning. It means getting the most done for the least amount of effort, money, and time.

The most efficient way to do the job is the safe way. Once the odds of getting hurt go up, the cost goes up, because, as all gamblers know, in the long run the house always wins. Taking chances with the safety or health of your people will never pay off—either in getting the work done or in winning their loyalty.

2. Get People to Work Together

This means cooperation, not intimidation. You cooperate with your work group, with your boss, with other managers in the company.

Sometimes managers develop a tight family feeling within their work group but are poor at cooperating with others in the company. The work group becomes like a cult and the manager the guru. All his attention is aimed inward, the perspective is narrow and he limits his growth potential within the company.

If, on the other hand, the manager neglects his group and pays too much attention to outsiders, the work of the group will decline in quality and quantity.

A good manager thinks in terms of what is best for the entire organization. He tries to balance the needs of his group with the needs of his boss and other managers in the company.

3. Develop and Maintain a Team Spirit

Morale and team spirit are important ingredients in any group. People have a hard time working for large, theoretical goals, like "profits" or "quality," when they don't experience them directly. They work harder for more immediate rewards, like praise, recognition, or the simple pleasure of pulling together as a group and getting something done that they could not do as individuals.

That's the essence of team spirit. It's exciting, it's rewarding, it's fun. It takes creative imagination and caring to develop. This means a blue ribbon on a desk, a silly sign on a bulletin board, a cake delivered by the local bakery. If you put yourself out just a little bit to show you care, you'll get it back in cooperation many times over.

4. Teach What You Know

A good manager spends a lot of time teaching. It's very hard to practice this because it doesn't seem immediately productive. It usually takes less time to do something yourself than to explain how to do it to someone else. But then you may have to do it a thousand times instead of explaining it only once.

The best manager devotes a lot of time developing people, passing along what he has learned so that others can move up as well. Employees want to grow, want to see themselves getting better at what they do. Yes, they are looking forward to their promotions, too. It's your job to help them. If you hold them back by not training them because they are too valuable to lose or if you hold them back because you are afraid they will surpass you, you are sure to lose them anyway.

Remember, the manager who trains a replacement is the best candidate for promotion.

5. Keep Good Records

There seem to be two types of people—the ones who hate paperwork of any kind and the ones who love it. The good manager recognizes which he is and does whatever is necessary to compensate.

If you hate paperwork, delegate it. Get somebody who likes writing and reading reports and records to do the job for you. You must supervise and always know what is going on, but you can limit the amount of time you spend doing this kind of work and still provide your boss and your successor with the data necessary to do their jobs.

If you love paperwork, discipline yourself to limit the time you spend at it. Assign a certain amount of time each day away from your desk or work station.

Balancing Responsibilities

It's obvious that you have a lot of balls to keep in the air at once.

You must balance

- the needs of the company with the needs of the individuals who report to you
- the need to get things done with the need to teach
- the need to maintain personal distance from employees with the need to be accessible and sympathetic
- the demands of the job against the human needs of the people who report to you

No one promised it was going to be easy.

CHAPTER 2.

How to Be a Leader

Look at a group of ants scurrying around. They don't seem to have a boss ant telling the others what they are supposed to be doing. Their jobs are programmed into their brains and they do them by instinct.

Throw a group of people into a pit and give them a task—even if it is just to get out of the pit—and they are going to get into each other's way until a leader appears.

"George, you get down on hands and knees. Harry, you kneel on top of George. OK, Mabel, up you go," and they're out.

We're not ants. We're complex creatures, each with a mind of his own, and for that reason we need a leader to help us achieve our goals.

Managers Manage People by Leading

We don't have a formula for leadership. It's an art, a craft, a knack, a talent. Some people have it naturally. Some people learn it. Some people never get the hang of it.

And some people couldn't care less about ever becoming a leader. Bless you, if you're one of those; close this book and give it to a friend.

Every Leader Is Different

Each eventually finds his own style. One will be dynamic, charismatic, electrifying. Another will be quiet, soft-spoken, reserved. Yet they can both be equally effective—win loyalty and get the job done just as fast and efficiently.

Despite the differences in style, there are a number of characteristics that are common to good leaders. You will recognize at least some of these qualities in the world's most famous leaders—in a Churchill or a John Kennedy, in Mahatma Gandhi and Jesus Christ. You may decide you are not ready to join this company, but if you have any ambitions of being a successful manager you will have to start somewhere.

A Leader Is Loyal

Loyalty is like money or affection: If you want to get it you have to invest some of your own.

Don't talk the company down to your employees. To them you *are* the company.

But that rule cuts both ways. Don't talk your employees down to your company if you expect them to deliver when you need them.

And you're going to need them.

A Leader Is an Optimist

The optimist is eager to listen to others and their ideas because he always expects good news. The pessimist listens as little as possible because he expects bad news.

The optimist thinks people are essentially helpful, creative, productive. The pessimist thinks they're lazy, resentful, wasteful. It's interesting that both these self-fulfilling prophecies usually prove correct.

The optimist gets up each morning with eager expectation and confidence. The pessimist would rather stay in bed.

The optimist welcomes the ideas of the people who work for him. To the pessimist new ideas are invariably a problem and they probably won't work anyway.

It's not surprising that the optimist moves up in the company; the pessimist stays right where he is.

A Leader Likes People

This is so obvious a characteristic it seems absurd to have to say it. If a manager's job is to manage people, how can he be good at it if he doesn't like people?

The best leaders care about people. They show a sincere interest in what others are doing, and this recognition makes people feel good about themselves and about the leader. They are approachable. They don't hide behind an office door.

The best leaders are human. They aren't any more perfect than the rest of us. They recognize their own weaknesses, which makes them more understanding of the weaknesses of others.

A Leader Is Courageous

Just a willingness to be out there in front of the pack already says something about the courage of a leader.

A leader will try a new way to do something just because it might be better.

A leader never says, "We don't do it that way," without a very good reason.

And if he lets someone try something and it doesn't work, a leader doesn't lose faith or lay blame. Without a willingness to pick yourself up and try again you'd never have learned to walk, tie your shoes, or ride a bicycle.

A Leader Looks over the Fences

A leader never says, "That's not my job." If you expect a team to pitch in when something unusual comes up you had better be ready to show them you're ready to pitch in when asked. When people refuse to do anything that is not in their job description, you can be sure you've got a company in serious trouble.

A leader has an immense interest in all aspects of company operations. He is curious about what other departments are doing and why. He asks questions, tries to be helpful—without making a pest of himself. If he is ever to move up in the company, he'll need to know more than the one group, department, or division.

A Leader Is Decisive

A leader is willing to make decisions, and if you don't think that takes courage, you don't know anything about being a manager.

When all the information is available, the correct decision is usually obvious. The tough decisions are when all the data isn't available, and a decision has to be made anyway. It takes real courage to make a decision and know that it could be wrong. Delay, indecisiveness, shilly-shallying are all clear messages that the manager is frightened, and no one respects or follows a frightened leader.

A Leader Is Tactful and Considerate

It's a simple fact of life—you get more from people with honey than with vinegar. Yet the seductive influence of power often makes us forget this fact. In our anxiety to get the job done we become impatient, intolerant, and inconsiderate of others' feelings. We ignore their suggestions, we deprecate their work, we shame them in front of their peers. We forget the cardinal rule, which is to criticize the work, not the person.

A wise man once said that every criticism should be made into a sandwich with the bread of praise on either side. The best leaders show their concern for people by making their communications tactful and considerate.

A Leader Is, Above All, Fair

When you make decisions about performance reviews, work assignments, promotions, pay increases, hiring, and firing, the entire group is affected. So it is important to be fair.

For example, if an employee gets a raise when he did nothing to deserve it you will probably have ten other disgruntled employees.

When an employee gets dressed down for something he didn't do, the morale of the entire group is affected.

When an employee makes a mistake, it should be brought to his attention, acknowledged by him, and then put aside.

Mistakes are opportunities to learn, not whips to beat the pride or self-respect out of people.

A Leader Is Honest

Honesty aimed upward tells upper-level managers things they might not want to hear. Honesty aimed downward tells employees when they've been wrong and when right. Honesty is when a manager admits his own mistakes.

It's not always easy to tell the truth without hurting feelings or seeming tactless, but honesty in the interests of the common good—the company or other people—should always be the primary goal.

A Leader Has Ambition

He is naturally ambitious for himself but the best leader is also ambitious for the people who report to him. He enjoys their successes and identifies with them. In this way he motivates others with his enthusiasm and energy and everyone moves up.

Note that like almost any quality, there can be too much of a good thing. Ambition that mows down anyone or anything in its path is destructive rather than productive.

Ambition aims at change, and many people are terrified of change. Pushing too hard can create more resistance than assistance, and the good leader knows when to slow down.

A leader always moves in high gear but appears to be just floating along. He favors the gentle push to the cracking whip, the carrot over the stick. A good leader is most of all a salesperson—selling ideas or plans of action to the people he reports to as much as to the people who report to him.

A Leader Is Consistent

Changing moods, irritability one day and euphoria the next, erratic and unpredictable responses to questions or emergencies, put a heavy burden on employees. To protect themselves they must always assume the worst—that the manager will overreact to a small error and probably ignore an important one.

The surest way to destroy morale, enthusiasm, spirit, and commitment is to constantly switch roles from dictator to charmer, from father to child, from optimist to pessimist. People won't know where you're coming from and eventually will stop trying to guess.

A Leader Is Humble

Strong leaders have a healthy self-image. They like the face they see in the mirror every morning. That being the case, they don't need flattery from others and they don't need to blow their own horns.

Conversely they don't need to cover up mistakes because they know that no one is perfect, least of all themselves—and that's OK.

People are never fooled by egotists. You wonder why they waste their time telling you how wonderful they are. The louder they boast, the more convinced we are of their insecurity and incompetence.

A Leader Is Self-confident

Self-confidence without arrogance, self-assurance without condescension, these are the earmarks of the strong leader.

There is a magnetism about people who are sure of themselves without having to say so. The simple appearance of confidence builds trust and a feeling of security in people who report to them. It also builds trust and security in the people who supervise them.

We all know that no one can be totally self-confident all the time. Where would the opportunity be for growth if the leader wasn't reaching beyond his grasp?

Who has the better chance of hitting a home run, the person who steps up to the plate thinking he will or the person who steps up thinking he won't?

A Leader Is a Teacher

We put it last in this list, but every major leader in history was first and foremost a teacher, and it is important to realize that the teaching goes beyond just the job at hand. The leader needs to transmit the skills of leadership as well. He helps his people develop self-confidence, a liking of people, ambition, enthusiasm, honesty, balance, decisiveness—all the things we have been discussing.

So how does a manager teach these leadership skills?

Think about the teachers who most influenced you in your life, whether in school, at home, on a playing field, in a job. It was someone who made you realize there was a bigger, more exciting, more interesting world out there than you originally thought. It was someone who made you solve problems yourself. He made you exercise and strengthen muscles you never knew you had, and so now you can apply those muscles to new problems or situations.

Too Big a Job?

You're right. You'd have to be a saint to have all the characteristics of a good leader.

If you were all those things you'd already be chairman of the board and certainly wouldn't have to read this book (though there are some board chairmen . . .).

But to get you started we've put together a list of things you can do to start in the right direction. They really aren't big-deal "assignments."

They are more like a slight shift in focus, a change in attitude so tiny you'll hardly notice. So small, in fact, that you may need a reminder now and then to keep at them, but give them a try at least for a while and see if the rewards aren't fantastic.

1. Become a People-Watcher

People are endlessly fascinating. If you
don't believe it, take a few moments every now
and then and study them.

2. Send out Inviting Vibes

Let people know you are interested in
them. Do it with your eyes, your body lan-
guage, any number of ways. Somehow let
them know you are sincerely interested.

3. Be Cordial

Say "Hello" as if you really mean it. Say
"How are you?" as if you really care. Smile.
Look them in the eye.

MONTROSE LIBRARY DISTRICT
434 SOUTH FIRST STREET
MONTROSE, COLORADO 81401

4. Boost an Ego

A job well done always deserves recognition and sometimes even a job partly well done earns some attention. It will cost you absolutely nothing to praise an employee and will return all kinds of unexpected dividends.

5. Admit Your Mistakes

We've said this before but it bears repeating. It will be seen as evidence of strength and power, not of weakness.

6. Get Yourself out of the Way

Take "I," "me," and "mine" out of your vocabulary for a day. This is an amazing exercise in self-control and may reveal something about yourself that you never suspected.

7. Visit with Your Team

They call this "management by walking around." This doesn't mean you hang out with them and appear to waste time. It does mean you make yourself available to hear their concerns, complaints, suggestions.

8. We're All Good Guys

Start the day thinking they'll be honest, they'll do it right the first time, there will be no indecisiveness, misrepresentation, backbiting. At least start the day that way.

CHAPTER 3.

How to Be a Teacher

It is so tempting to neglect the training responsibilities you have as a manager. You are busy, there is a pile of work with a deadline looming, your people are reasonably competent as it is; who has time to worry about what they *could* be trained to do?

Often, too, it will seem easier to do it yourself and get it right the first time than to let someone else do it and risk botching the job.

Wouldn't it be great to have the reputation as the person in the company who develops superstars? Then everyone with ambition or talent will want to work for *you.*

Remember, <u>credit multiplies, blame divides.</u>

Don't Pass the Buck

You are not off the hook just because the company already has a formal training program. In such programs, people usually learn theory and basic skills. The application of the theory and the practice of those skills is your responsibility. Without the application and reinforcement, the classroom training is a waste.

Most people don't learn and integrate new information from a lecture or a demonstration. They have to do it themselves, make the mistakes, see the results in front of them, before the skill becomes theirs.

The Rewards of Training

The benefits of a conscious effort to teach are immediate and bountiful:

- People produce better work
- They produce more work
- They are happier because they feel respected and appreciated
- Happy people don't get sick so often
- They don't quit
- They don't sit around wondering what they are supposed to be doing
- You will soon find yourself with time to plan, to be creative

How People Learn

Learning is a change that happens when a person responds physically and mentally to external stimuli. The more senses that are stimulated, the more likely the change will take place.

For example, tell an employee how to do something and he only utilizes one sense—hearing. Tell and show someone at the same time and we have two senses in action and the information is twice as likely to stick.

The more pronounced and varied the stimulation, the better are the chances for learning. Try to use colorful visual aids, vivid demonstrations, dramatic presentations that combine sound, sight, and some action, or physical participation of the audience.

The Principles of Learning

A lot of research has been done about how people learn, and from this information we have distilled the following guidelines.

These may be extremely helpful in designing on-the-job training programs for your employees. You may also find them useful when you are learning something on your own.

1. People Learn When They Are Ready

They have to *want* to learn, and that means you may need to supply an incentive of some kind. Incentives are of two kinds—carrot or stick.

The carrot incentive goes like this:

<u>If you learn this</u> you'll be more skilled, the job will be easier to do, you can take more responsibility and make more money, you'll eventually get promoted, and so forth.

The stick incentive goes like this:

<u>If you don't learn this</u> you will have an accident and hurt yourself, you'll never get a raise or a promotion, you will get fired, and so forth.

2. People Like to Do What They Do Well

Our attitudes toward learning start in childhood. Some children are encouraged to try new things—are picked up when they fall, dusted off, hugged, and turned loose to try again. These people have many experiences of getting past the failures to enjoy the successes. They are easy to teach because they are ready and open.

Others were not given that kind of loving encouragement. Their experience is if they try to do something new they will fail, period. They need lots of strokes.

The way to handle them is to give them the information in tiny packets that can't fail. In this way there is very little risk and each step moves them, almost imperceptibly, from not having a skill to having it.

3. Practice, Practice, Practice

- The more often you do it the better you get at it.
- The better you get at it the more often you will do it.
- The more often you do it the better you get at it.
- The better you get at it the more often you will do it.
- And so on.

4. Friendly Competition Speeds Learning

For some people *any* competition makes them try harder, apply themselves more. But for most of us the competition should be friendly, the peer pressure gentle.

It is also preferable to have the competition be against oneself. <u>When an employee competes against himself there are no losers.</u>

5. Learning Moves in Fits and Starts

The learning curve isn't a curve at all, but a staircase. You step up to a new level and then seem to sit there forever.

Sports provide the most familiar experience of this. You are trying to learn a new golf swing or a stronger tennis serve and for months it seems you play at a given level and then one day you have a dramatic improvement in speed, distance, accuracy.

You have to encourage employees, and yourself, to stick it out through the plateaus, knowing that the next step will be reached in its own good time.

6. It Takes Both Sender and Receiver

Teacher and student share the responsibility for what happens. If you are the teacher it will be tempting to blame slow learning on the student. If you are the student it will be tempting to blame your problems on the teacher.

Both participants have equal responsibility for progress. If either fails, both fail.

7. Divide the Material into Steps

A student needs positive and frequent feedback. That means the information should be divided into bites that can be absorbed in a reasonably short period of time and immediately applied either to actual work tasks or to preparation for the next bite.

The idea is to give the student a reward and a sense of accomplishment at each step.

8. Make the Classroom Comfortable

Whether it is a classroom or simply the place where the teaching takes place, it should be possible for the student to focus on the task and not have to sit on a hard seat, feel too hot or too cold, have to struggle to hear over distracting noise, and so forth.

If a student is physically uncomfortable you have lost the battle for his attention.

10. Do Your Homework

Be sure you know exactly what it is you want to teach. For example, do you want him to learn the entire bookkeeping system or just how to post numbers in the ledger?

- What does he already know?
- How much can he absorb in any one session? (The mind can only comprehend what the seat can endure.)
- Put the bite-size chunks of data in logical sequence.
- Keep a record of where you are in the sequence so you don't lose your place or wander into unknown territory.
- Practice before each session, at least in your mind and preferably before someone.
- Have all necessary equipment or materials prepared and the location arranged for in advance.
- Look at the information from the student's point of view.

11. When the Big Day Comes

- Get the student to relax. A tense mind will be too preoccupied to learn anything.
- Show and tell—but *slowly*. Remember how confusing it was when *you* first started.
- Don't be impatient with slow learners—it's the surest way to blow the whole session.
- Have him perform the task with you and then by himself.
- Flash the carrot every now and then to keep the incentive in the forefront of his mind.
- Correct errors at once. Don't wait until the entire sequence has been completed. Immediate feedback reinforces learning.
- Show respect. Don't be condescending, stern, or harsh. A person is very vulnerable in a learning situation.
- Give him some time to practice alone and let him know where he can get help if needed.
- Check up on his technique from time to time to make sure he doesn't develop bad habits.

CHAPTER 4.

Boundaries and Direction

By *boundaries* we mean what is and what is not acceptable behavior on the job.

By *direction* we mean how orders are given and the discipline that establishes who is in charge and what exactly is expected of people.

Without structure and boundaries you have anarchy, which will not be appreciated either by your superiors or by the people who report to you.

Most people become uncomfortable without structure. It tells them exactly what they are supposed to be doing and when. They don't have to second-guess the boss. Most important, they know what differentiates a job well done from one that is marginal, sloppy, or downright unacceptable.

Look for Talent and Use It

The first step is to assign the right person to the right job, and that's your responsibility. Either people come to you qualified to do the job or you have to train them.

Often you will find talents among your people that are not listed in their job descriptions or their personnel files. As we said earlier, people like to do what they do well; conversely, people do well what interests them.

Sometimes people are not even aware that they have particular talents. This is one of the great rewards of being a manager—helping employees discover their own talents.

Work on Their Weaknesses

When an employee is not performing as expected it's the manager's responsibility to find out why. The trick here will be to get behind the alibis and discover the real problem.

If it's *carelessness*, you have to try to instill some pride.

If it's *nervousness*, you have to instill self-confidence.

If it's *ignorance*, you have to teach.

Direct your attention to the *cause* of the problem, not its symptoms. Ask yourself what you can do differently to help the employee do the job. Build on the person's strengths; don't harp incessantly on the weaknesses.

Suit the Job to the Personality

To make the point clear let's look at the extremes:

An extrovert likes to work with people. Put an extrovert in an office by himself and you have two problems—the job won't get done and you've wasted a talent.

An introvert likes to work alone. Give him paperwork, correspondence, numbers, and he'll be a powerhouse. Put him among people and he's a wallflower.

Nervous, high-strung people need a quiet environment. Put them in a noisy, hectic office and they overload and blow a fuse.

Motivated, intelligent people have no patience for repetitive, noncreative work. They are self-starters who need to be given challenges that stretch and exercise their abilities.

Orders: The Command

There are two things to be considered when deciding how to give a work order:

- The situation. Do you have the time to use subtlety?
- The person. Is this a conscientious high achiever or someone who needs to be pushed and prodded at every step?

The <u>command</u> is the simplest and most direct:

<u>"Do this because I said so!"</u>
You will automatically use it in an emergency: "Call an ambulance!"

You will also need to use it with the careless, lazy employee whose resistance is high and whose attention span is limited.

Orders: The Request

If the work is routine and the manager/employee relationship is trusting and comfortable, the request will probably work best.

"Would you please do this?" This gives the employee an opening to say why it can't be done, if that is the case, or why it might not be a good idea. It may protect you, the manager, against a disastrous error and pays lip service to the employee's freedom of choice.

If phrased correctly you can be sure there will be no doubt in the employee's mind that it is an order.

Orders: The Question

When you want to actively solicit criticism on how a job should be done or want to nudge an employee into taking the initiative, you use the question.

"Would it be a good idea to do this?"

Note you are suggesting a direction or method and you are asking for comments. A more extreme example would be:

"How should we do this?" or even

"Should we do this?"

It is the best way to give orders to highly motivated self-starters because the job becomes a team effort in which they share in the planning and thinking as well as the doing.

Dangers in the Question

The question entails some risks:

1. Some employees are too insecure to hear it as a question. They assume a question is a command and will go ahead and do it no matter how absurd the consequences.

2. Some employees are out to get you and will take great pleasure in following instructions which they assume are implied through a question, just to make you look like a fool.

3. Some employees may take this as a sign of weakness and ignore you entirely because it wasn't phrased as an order.

Orders: The Volunteer

This is for the job no one wants to do but that has to be done.

<u>"Who wants to do this?"</u>

If you give a direct order for the unpleasant job you may get a lot of moaning and groaning or resentment from someone who feels picked on. A volunteer, however, hopes his willingness will be remembered when salary-review time comes around.

A caution: Eager employees tend to be volunteers and may be resented by others who are more reserved but equally loyal or conscientious.

Giving the Specifics

Employees are not mind readers; on the other hand, you don't want to insult them by giving them too much detail. Treading the fine line between respecting their intelligence and giving them everything they need to do the job requires that *you* have a good understanding of their competence and prior knowledge.

Review what is important about this task by going down the mental checklist of

- What?
- Why?
- Who?
- Where?
- When?
- How?

Do You Need to Say Who?

You could say, "Mary, please get someone to help you with the cost analysis you're doing so that you can finish by tomorrow."

Mary has no authority over other workers. She asks Beth, who is lazy, or Arthur, who is working on another priority project, and gets turned down.

A better way to phrase this would be, "Mary, please get Sue to help you with the cost analysis you're doing so that you can finish by tomorrow."

Do You Need to Say When?

You say, "John, please call the accounting department about the incorrect billing of this customer."

John has a desk full of other tasks and waits a week to make the call. In the meantime the customer is in a rage, wondering why your accounting department keeps dunning him.

A better way would have been "John, please call the accounting department immediately about the incorrect billing of this customer."

Other Things to Consider

- Is the order necessary? Don't ask someone to do a meaningless job.
- Do you have the authority? You'll save yourself some embarrassment if you don't go beyond your authority either with the person or with the nature of the order.
- Get to the point. Don't make a speech and don't bury the order in a mass of irrelevant material, or the employee won't remember that there even was an order in all that talk.
- Practice the five C's. Give the order: Clearly, Completely, Concisely, Confidently, and Correctly.
- Put it in writing. If the order is complicated or long, write it out. The human mind can hold only a limited number of things at once.

Follow Up

This takes a fine managerial sense of the employee and his capability.

If you follow up in detail on every order you give you show disrespect and a lack of trust in the employee. He will feel insulted.

On the other hand, if you have any doubts about whether the employee understands the order you must check to see if the job was done and done correctly. This speaks to your role as teacher as well as responsible manager.

When They Fail

If the employee doesn't do what he is told, you must let him know you are aware of it or else he will think he's put one over on you. If you don't hand out a necessary reprimand you are not doing your job.

- Get all the facts. Be sure you know everything you need to know before reprimanding.
- Plan your approach. Decide beforehand what you are going to say and how you are going to say it.
- Start by asking the employee why it happened or didn't happen. He may have data you don't have that explains it all.
- Do it in private. Dignity and self-respect must be honored. The reprimanded employee shouldn't have to worry about his peers as well as you.

- Tailor the reprimand to the person and the problem. A sensitive, insecure employee will react strongly to the barest hint of criticism. The tough, careless one may need to be raked over the coals.
- If it is appropriate, use the sandwich technique—put a criticism between two compliments.
- Don't lose your temper. Show your anger if you must, but in a quiet rather than roof-raising manner.
- Direct the criticism at the behavior, not the person.
- Get the employee to admit the error, if possible, and then end the discussion quickly.
- Don't threaten. He should understand that what's past is past, but in the future such errors will be taken more seriously.
- End on a friendly note and find an opportunity soon after to have an I'm-not-mad-anymore conversation with the person.

Motivation and Incentives

In the best of all worlds employees are motivated to work hard and well and require no externally applied discipline. They feel important, are treated with respect, and give the company their best in return.

It is your job to build this spirit of cooperation.

There will be individuals who won't become members of the team, who won't share in the high morale. You may have to put them on probation or even fire them. This should always be done carefully and with respect and concern for the employee.

Negative Discipline

Threats and punishment should be used very rarely, if at all. Remember that employees have as many ways to retaliate as you have to punish. Negative discipline brings out the worst in people. It makes them frightened or angry—hardly the best atmosphere in which to get productive, high-quality work.

The biggest motivation killer is when a manager is inconsistent in enforcing rules or when employees are allowed to be idle and unproductive. They lose self-respect as well as respect for you the manager and, ultimately, for the company.

It comes down to caring. When a manager appreciates and values employees, when he has their interest and welfare at heart, when he respects them as individuals, there should be little need for negative discipline.

Tips on Handling People

- Set a good example. Don't expect them to obey rules if you don't.
- Treat them as individuals. No two people are alike.
- Be fair. Never play favorites.
- Treat them as if they belong. A bonding takes place among team members and then peer pressure will bring out their best.
- Don't ration information. Tell them what they need to do the job and maybe just a little more so that they understand how their job fits into the whole. Deal with rumors at once.
- Use authority sparingly. You don't need to impress them with your power.
- Delegate. Give them responsibility and get it off your back.

More Tips

- Respond appropriately. Don't overreact to little problems or ignore big ones.
- Trust the employees. Expect the best (and allow for occasional disappointment).
- Make sure they are trained. You can't expect them to do what they haven't been trained to do.
- Admit your own mistakes. Employees usually find out anyway, and denying mistakes is a display of weakness.
- Be loyal. Loyalty begets loyalty. What goes around comes around.
- Don't let them be idle. Plan tasks for the quiet times as well as the busy ones.

CHAPTER 5.

Team Building

If the <u>what</u> of the manager's job is to get certain tasks done, the <u>how</u> is through team building.

Getting people to work together has to be one of the most demanding and exasperating tasks a manager has to face.

People aren't born believing it is their job to sacrifice life and limb for the company. By earning their respect, a good leader turns a group of people into a team that pulls together and produces.

Two conflicting emotions are at work here:

- People need to feel part of a group. It gives them security, affection, a kind of love.
- People need to be individuals. They want to be respected for who they are and feel distinctive.

When Teamwork Isn't There

Certainly competition is normal. Ambitious people will compete for attention, for promotions, for another step up the corporate ladder. But jealousy, hostility, and politics are the concomitants of competition and most group tasks will suffer when employees compete as individuals rather than as a team.

Watch for these symptoms:

- Questions from other departments are handled sloppily or not at all
- You hear repeatedly "That's not my job"
- Conversations are gossipy and snide and unrelated to the work
- Absenteeism is high
- Faces are blank or sullen rather than smiling and welcoming
- Voices sound whiny
- The outsider is treated as an interruption rather than an important part of the day
- Turnover is high

Why People Join Teams

A group offers psychological and material rewards. The more the group satisfies these needs, the more powerful and long-lived it will be.

- Security. It is a place where members can feel safe, cared for.
- Belonging. It provides an identification.
- Individuality. The group recognizes and supports the valuable differences of its members.
- Pride. Members share in group achievements.
- Recognition. The outside world respects the group as a more powerful entity than it would an individual.

Successful managers know how to create and nurture groups. They are sowers of pride.

Overcoming Resistance to Change

People *hate* a change that is not a clear and demonstrable improvement in money or working conditions. At the least, change is disturbing, frightening. The optimist strains to find something good about change; the pessimist knows it will be disastrous.

- Get employees' help in formulating changes. People will support what they help create.
- Consider how the change will look to *them.*
- Provide lots of advance notice so they can get used to the idea.
- Make changes very slowly and in small steps.
- Be careful about timing; two changes at the same time are four times as bad as one.

Distributing Work Fairly

Very often managers don't distribute work evenly because some people are more competent than others. "Give the job to Mary, she'll do it in no time and I know it will be done right. Give it to John and he'll be in here with a dozen questions, it'll take a week, and I'll have to do it over myself."

So Mary gets all the work and soon burns out while John is underloaded and has plenty of idle time to make mischief.

Training is the great equalizer.

Favoritism and Familiarity

We wrote earlier about the dangers of favoritism. It is obviously destructive of team spirit.

A good manager also draws a careful line between friendliness and familiarity. Friendliness can be applied equally to everyone on the team. Familiarity suggests a special relationship that destroys the appearance of impartiality if not the actuality.

If you want to keep their respect, <u>don't ever let your employees see you out of control.</u>

Setting an Example

If you ever want to jerk an employee's chain, make him abide by rules you consistently violate. Come to work late, leave early, take two-hour lunches, make personal calls. Adults, like kids, are extraordinarily adept at picking up bad habits.

This doesn't mean you can't come in late if you worked until two in the morning—but you would give the employee the same privilege, wouldn't you?

Sharing Credit

Good managers always give credit where credit is due. Super managers give credit to the team even when the manager was largely responsible for the success.

Managers who steal ideas and adopt them as their own create enemies and cut off the flow of future ideas.

How to Handle Personal Problems

If you are a sympathetic manager you become a father or mother figure to employees and they may bring personal problems to you. Even if they don't come cry on your shoulder, you may be aware that something is interfering with their work.

Tempting as it may be, <u>never tell an employee what to do about his personal problems.</u> If it works you won't get the credit. If it doesn't it will be your fault.

Listen, nod sympathetically, make a few general observations. It's probably best not even to ask questions, which can seem probing and invasive. The goal is to calm the hysteria, dry the tears. If the problem seems chronic and serious, direct the employee to professional counselors who specialize in the problem.

Cooperating Upward

Knowing how to manage your boss is as important as managing the people who report to you. You can make him an ally or an enemy.

Here the golden rule applies with double strength. <u>Do unto your boss as you would have your subordinate do unto you.</u>

- Be loyal.
- Be dependable.
- Neither a yes-man nor a no-man be. The employee who always says yes is superfluous. The employee who always says no is a constant irritant.
- Never try to boss your boss. Make suggestions tactfully. You can't give him a direct order but you can say, "Don't you think it would be a good idea if . . . ?"

- Keep your boss informed. Nothing irritates a manager more than to have outsiders know more about what is happening in his department than he does. Keep the boss advised of personnel problems, the status of projects, proposed changes, budgets, and other important matters. Let him know about disasters early and try to have solutions ready at the same time.
- Present completed work. Try to get the work as close to finished as possible, even though you suspect he will want to revise it completely himself. He doesn't want to hear from you at every step. If you were he, would you stake your reputation on this work?
- Last, but not least, remember, he is trying to build a team, too.

Cooperating Sideways

Finding the right way to cooperate with peers is bound to be difficult. These are the people you are competing with for advancement, yet these are the people who make up your boss's team.

- Try to create clear separation of authority. Overlapping functions are the most dangerous. If your boss won't do it, you must try.
- Don't pass the buck. If one of your employees screws up, take the blame yourself.
- Be careful when lending or borrowing employees. Don't send your lead-bottomed losers—they'll think your whole team is like that and you may get the same treatment in return.

Observe the Chain of Command

This applies from the top down as much as it does from bottom up.

You don't go around your manager to <u>his</u> manager without a very good reason. Similarly, a boss should not countermand the order given by a subordinate except in dire emergency. First, there may be a good reason why the subordinate gave the order that is not apparent on the surface. Second, the subordinate loses face, authority, credibility—all things painfully won and essential in the effort to build a team.

The boss should transmit such orders <u>through</u> the subordinate even at the cost of a few hours' work.

Delegation of Responsibility

Nothing does more for team building than the proper delegation of responsibility. As usual, it must be done in moderation and with care, but allowing the employees to make decisions, to deal with their problems by themselves, to suggest and implement changes, takes the load off the manager and gives the employees a sense of participation that is created in no other way.

All routine tasks and decisions should be delegated.

By this we mean all jobs or questions that are repetitive or can be reduced to a formula should be handled by someone other than the manager. The manager formulates the response the first time and then lets someone else make it.

This applies even if it means that someone else will be representing the group to higher-ups.

Delegation of Authority

The single biggest complaint by managers at all levels is when a manager delegates responsibility without also delegating the necessary authority.

Why do managers do this? It's simply because they are afraid to let loose the reins of control.

They understand they can't do everything themselves, that employees need more involvement in decision making, that they must delegate to build team spirit and morale, that they must stop being the corporate bottleneck. But they fear that giving up authority will reduce their power.

Delegation works from the top down. If you find a mid-level manager who is not delegating enough you can be sure that there will be managers below him who are likewise not delegating enough.

When this occurs, a higher-level manager must step in and delicately point out what is happening.

Giving Reasons Why

Another frequent error made by managers is not telling employees what is going on. The crew is supposed to swab the deck and not worry about where the ship is going. Again we are dealing with a manager's fear. He sees knowledge as power and the sharing of knowledge as reduction in his power.

The solution is gentle pressure from above. "Have you told your staff about this?" shows the manager that the dissemination of information is considered part of his job.

For major decisions that affect many employees a more direct solution is to make a prompt announcement through company-wide memos or, better yet, to tell people personally either in staff meetings or one on one. The key word here is prompt. Don't let the rumor mill carry a distorted version through the company two days before the memo.

Remember, most rumors start at the copying machine.

CHAPTER 6.

How to Handle Complaints

There are bound to be employee grumbles, gripes, frets, and fumes, and it is part of the manager's job to handle them.

It is tempting to ignore complaints as petty time-wasters and many will seem childish and inane. But remember, complaints are important to *them* even though they may not seem that way to you, so you must never treat them as trivial.

Curiously, employees don't quit because they have a complaint; they quit because the complaint wasn't heard and respected. That's an insult to them personally and will not be tolerated.

Do you see the difference? <u>You don't always have to solve the problem but you do always have to listen to it described.</u>

Most companies have an administrative procedure to handle complaints, but complaints aren't solved by procedures, they are solved by managers.

Complainers Aren't Disloyal

It is a mistake to assume that someone who complains about a situation hates the company, the management, or you.

Nothing could be further from the truth.

It is entirely possible that the complainer is doing you a big favor by letting you know of a situation that others are suffering with in silence. Silent suffering is an acid that burns holes in the stomach and destroys productive energy.

Seen in this light, complaints deserve your gratitude, not retaliation.

What Is a Complaint?

It is anything that rubs an employee the wrong way or makes his work difficult or unpleasant. Let's review the major areas of complaint:

- Salaries: base pay not high enough, paid holidays, overtime, you name it. <u>This is the critical one. Never be casual about an employee's paycheck.</u>
- Working conditions. This is the largest category. It consists of everything from a request for a softer chair to a production line that runs too fast.
- Relationships within the department. This is usually a difference between individuals. It's difficult to handle because it almost always involves two wrongs, not one.
- Relationships with other departments. This can be a conflict with an individual in another department or a procedural problem.

How to Handle Complaints

- Try to anticipate problems and avoid setting up situations that will trigger complaints. To be successful at this you must put yourself in the employees' shoes and imagine how the situation seems to them.
- Welcome the complaint. If you can't give the employee the time at the moment make an appointment at a time when you can.
- Listen first. Don't reject the complaint out of hand—that denies the employee's real feeling of grievance. On the surface the employee comes to you for action but often he will be satisfied with a sympathetic ear.
- Listen to both sides. If the complaint concerns another employee on the team or another department make sure you hear the other's side.
- If you are going to act, act promptly. If you are not going to act, tell the employee why. At the least, the employee wants to feel heard and three weeks of silence makes the whole effort seem pointless.

When You Can't Resolve the Problem

It may not be in your power to eliminate the cause of the complaint because it involves a matter at a higher level or goes against company policy.

The problem then has to be kicked upstairs or to an ombudsman individual or group. <u>The complaint then becomes yours.</u> You are the channel through which it flows to your manager, or your manager's manager.

If the Problem Concerns YOU

This takes enormous patience and self-control. Some mechanism must exist that allows employees the privilege of going over a manager's head to make a complaint. It may be as simple as your giving permission for the employee to do so. You must warn your manager that the complaint is coming, brief him about its content, and then step back and let him handle it.

If *you* are the manager in this situation <u>you owe first loyalty to the manager who is being bypassed,</u> and only if there is clear justice in the complaint will you step in and overrule an order or make a change.

CHAPTER 7.

How to Hire

Almost all companies have a personnel department that does the initial screening but it stands to reason that they can only do so if you provide them with enough information to do it intelligently.

It's a question of balance. You want them to pass along a good candidate even though he may not have the background education or experience that seems necessary. On the other hand, you don't want to waste time interviewing candidates who are not suited for the job.

So initially, as well as ultimately, the responsibility for getting good people for your team is yours.

The personnel department should be able to deliver people with the right qualifications. You must decide whether the chemistry is right among the candidate, yourself, and your team.

Experience

Some things to watch for:

- Too many job changes. More than one job in any one year should send up warning flares in your head. Preferably you would like someone with at least two or three years in each position.
- Glowing descriptions of accomplishments. Probe these in the interview to satisfy yourself that they aren't grossly exaggerated.
- Meaningless titles. Ask what were the actual duties in each job. You can't assume that a title in another company means the same that it does in yours.
- Previous salaries. Salary is probably a better indicator of responsibility than title, though different industries have different levels of remuneration.

Remember that, depending on the job, experience isn't always necessary and may actually be a disadvantage if you hope to train this person to do it your way.

Intelligence and Education

Suit the person to the job. If you put over-qualified people into low-level jobs you are going to have dissatisfied employees and a lot of turnover.

Conversely, don't put underqualified people into a position where, even with considerable effort, they will not be able to do the job. You'll have frustrated them as well as yourself.

Book learning is rarely directly applicable to a job and it may give the candidate an unwarranted belief in his own capabilities. Common sense and a willingness to learn are almost always more valuable than formal education.

Appearance

You have a right to expect any candidate to come to an interview looking neat and well groomed. This indicates pride in oneself and provides at least an indication that his work will be neat as well.

If he doesn't come to an interview looking presentable he sure won't look any better when he shows up for the job.

Conversely, just because he comes to the interview looking like an IBM salesperson, you can't assume that's the way he will look on the job.

Adaptability

You may not have thought of this but it is a very important personality characteristic. Rigidity and inflexibility are tough problems to deal with because they leave no room for growth and change.

Personality

They don't have to win a popularity contest but:

- Is the person tactful, poised, self-confident?
- Is the person easy to talk to?
- Does the person seem likely to get along with others in the group?
- Is this a loner, or someone who likes to work with other people?

Try to ask questions for which a pat answer wouldn't have been prepared. Take into account nervousness; in some cases it won't matter, though in others it may be critically important.

Age, Sex, Race, and So Forth

Put these at the bottom of the list of factors—for practical as well as legal reasons. Today women and younger people are holding positions that were unheard of ten years ago.

Older people, too, are returning to the job market and are proving to be extremely desirable employees. They are by definition more mature, they are more stable, have fewer accidents, tend toward less absenteeism, and are less likely to switch jobs.

Legally, the Equal Employment Opportunity Act forbids discrimination because of race, creed, color, sex, age, or origin. If a candidate suspects that he was rejected because of discrimination, your company may be on the receiving end of a costly suit.

CHAPTER 8.

Interviewing Techniques

You are about to make a decision you may have to live with for years. Don't do it lightly. An interview with a candidate requires preparation.

- Keep in the forefront of your mind the position that is to be filled.
- Take the time to read the résumé before the interview. It helps to make better use of your time.
- Know what questions you want to ask. If you don't, the candidate may wind up interviewing *you.*
- Put yourself in the proper frame of mind. If you are tired or irritable you can't do the candidate justice.
- Plan to give him your undivided attention. This is an important decision that you are making. Eliminate interruptions, calls, and so forth.
- Choose a place that provides quiet, privacy, and comfort.

Your Attitude

- Be impartial. As far as possible put aside your prejudices. First impressions are dictated by prejudice and may be totally off base.
- Make sure the candidate knows who you are—name *and* title.
- Use the candidate's name early and frequently in the interview.
- Think of the candidate as an interesting person from whom you can learn something—at the very least who you *don't* want for this job.
- Seek a common ground, a place where your interests and the candidate's coincide. This builds confidence and will encourage him to reveal himself to you.
- Smile. Be friendly. A frightened candidate can't show you his good points.
- Treat the candidate the way you would like to be treated if the roles were reversed.

Give the Facts

You are responsible for making sure the candidate gets all the facts and understands them.

- Review the facts about the position—its good points as well as bad. This includes job requirements, hours, working conditions, job security, opportunities for advancement, employee benefits, and rate of pay.
- Speak slowly and clearly. Make sure he has time to absorb what you have said. This is a high-stress situation for the candidate and he may find it hard to listen.
- Make no promises you can't keep. Don't exaggerate the opportunities for advancement. If they aren't there a disappointed employee will be resentful.

The Questions

Make sure the candidate does more talking than you do. Remember, <u>you are interviewing him, he is not interviewing you.</u> A clever candidate can get you talking and you may wind up with a glowing opinion of him when all you heard was yourself.

- Keep questions clear and concise. Don't use trick questions.
- Ask one question at a time.
- Start with the easy ones and save the probing ones for later.
- Ask questions about what he has done, what he wants to do, what he can do, what he will do.

More Questions

- Ask questions that don't have obvious answers. (<u>Not:</u> Are you hardworking? Do you get along with others?) He will try to psyche out the answers you want to hear. Don't make it too easy.
- Cross-check answers by asking similar questions phrased differently later on.
- Ask open-ended questions that require more than yes or no answers.
- Pay attention to the questions he asks you. Do they indicate the kind of person you want to have on your team?

What You Want to Learn

- Is the candidate industrious or lazy?
- Will the candidate be loyal or only care about himself?
- Is the candidate alert?
- Is the candidate open-minded or stubborn and opinionated?
- Is the candidate observant?
- Is the candidate a self-starter or need specific orders?
- Does the candidate enjoy learning new things?
- Is the candidate enthusiastic?
- Does the candidate have common sense?
- Is the candidate honest in small things and large?
- Why did the candidate really leave the last job?
- Is the candidate thorough in his work (and take forever to get finished) or quick and dirty?
- Does the candidate take pride in what he does?

What to Look For

- Don't let the résumé influence your opinion too much. There's usually more (or less) to a person than you will find on one or two sheets of paper.
- Listen with all your senses. Nonverbal communication is at least as important as verbal. What is the candidate telling you by his facial expression, hand motions, body position, eye contact?
- Answers often provide information in areas quite distant from the immediate subject. For example, someone who hang-glides tells you he likes risk; if he built his own house he has staying power and likes to work with his hands.
- The candidate is nervous. He may sweat, grin too much, have shaky hands. Unless cool under fire is a necessary characteristic for the job, nervousness should have little bearing on his qualifications.

The Conclusion

- Try to give immediate feedback, at least as far as his chances in getting the job. Don't raise his hopes if he has no chance. Without destroying his self-respect, tell him why his chances of getting the job are slim.
- Regardless of the outcome, make him feel a little better for having interviewed for this job. Raise his self-esteem with a compliment.
- Smile, shake hands, wish him luck.

CHAPTER 9.

How to Orient the New Recruit

You interviewed him. You hired him. It's your responsibility to get him started. Certainly there are many aspects of the original orientation that can be delegated to others—you don't have to fill out all the payroll information and you don't have to tell him how to operate the phone system—but it is your responsibility to introduce him to his co-workers, explain to them and to him what his job is, and give him his initial work assignments.

Remember that the new employee is not just a replacement cog to be inserted into the machine. He is an individual who merely by his presence will shift the center of gravity of the entire group. He takes on the group culture, but influences the culture as well.

The Impact of Change

When a new employee joins the company it means change, change for current employees and change for the new person. In some organizations, particularly where there are a lot of long-term employees, there is a clannishness that may be actively hostile to the new person. Hostility is caused by fear—fear that the new employee will outshine the others, fear that he will do things differently.

Obviously the new person is also afraid. These are people he is going to have to work with forty hours a week, fifty-two weeks a year. He senses that there are political currents and has to be extremely careful about making wrong moves, aligning himself with the wrong clique.

The manager's job is to allay the fears as much as possible, which means to reassure the old employees and provide support to the new one.

First Impressions

What do you want the new employee to learn in those first few days? Who is to be his chief instructor? First impressions are lasting and, if wrong, difficult to change. Further, if the manager doesn't take the time to get the new employee started, the employee has to think he isn't very important to the operation. If he doesn't feel important to the company, the company won't be very important to him.

Poor indoctrination results in:

- a long adjustment period
- mistakes, mistakes, mistakes
- low productivity
- costly grievances
- increased turnover
- increased costs

The Formal Orientation

Every employee should attend a formal orientation conducted by the company. The program explicitly provides the basic information about company-wide policy and procedure and implicitly shows the new employee how the company sees itself and how it wishes to be regarded by the surrounding community of customers, suppliers, and competitors.

The program should take the first steps toward instilling pride in the new employee. He should be made to feel part of something important. Today we hear a lot of complaints about the declining work ethic, but people will take pride in their work only if they feel pride in their company.

Companies spend millions of dollars on sophisticated marketing programs directed at customers and then totally ignore their own employees. How can employees be expected to deliver what the marketing programs promise?

What the Company Should Say

The formal orientation should include information about:

- company history
- organizational structure
- functions of various departments
- management philosophy regarding customers and employees
- company products or services
- what is expected of employees
- employee benefits

Who speaks is just as important as what is said. If a senior officer of the corporation takes the time to give the orientation to employees they know they are important.

What YOU Say

The formal orientation program introduces the employee to the company; the manager introduces the employee to the department and the job.

Note that toward the end of the first day the new employee is sure to look like he's about to fall apart. Give him an understanding word or two but don't worry. He has been overloaded with new people and job instructions and can't be expected to integrate them all in one day.

How to Break the Ice

- Put him at ease. A smile and a welcoming handshake will go a long way to help him through a difficult time.
- You don't need to impress him with *your* importance. Call him by his first name and use it several times in your conversation with him.
- While he is with you, give him your undivided attention. Show a personal interest in him. Discuss subjects you know from the interview were of mutual interest.
- Do not criticize the company. Show him you are proud of the company and your work group, that the group contributes to the well-being of the company and that you do good work and are proud of it.

Be Careful of Information Overkill

The new employee doesn't want to wait two or three weeks before he finds out exactly what he's supposed to do. He wants to know on day one. Put the work in the perspective of overall company objectives. Make sure he realizes the job he does is important to the company and to you, his manager.

Give him the minimum essential information he needs to do the job—no more. It's easy to overwhelm a new employee by feeding him everything you know about the job in the first few minutes. It took you months, if not years, to learn it all. Have a heart.

Policies, Procedures, Standards

Spell out exactly what is expected of the new employee. If you don't tell him the rules he either learns from others and repeats their mistakes or makes them up.

- What time is he expected to arrive for work?
- If he drives to work, where does he park?
- What is quitting time?
- How much time for lunch and when?
- What about overtime as it applies to his job?
- How do vacations get assigned?
- Who does he notify if he is sick?
- Are there specific office procedures that differ from what he was told in the company orientation?

Give Him a Road Map

An employee needs to know where things are:

- his office
- rest rooms
- your office
- company lunch rooms or nearby restaurants
- nurse's office
- personnel office for information on benefits, vacation, and so forth

Introduce Him to Fellow Employees

It's your responsibility to introduce the new employee to the people he will be working with. <u>Do not delegate this</u> to your secretary or whoever happens to pass by at the moment.

Each brief conversation must exchange names and titles or job functions and something good about the person being introduced. This gives him a hint as to how he will be treated in the future. He probably won't remember the names of all the people he meets or what they do, but the ones important to his job should stick and the others can be learned later.

It takes a diplomatic touch to give both the old employees and the new one the reassurance they need to calm fears generated by the change.

Depending on his personality it may be helpful to suggest that someone lunch with the new employee for the first day or two.

Touch base with him at the end of the first day and once or twice during the next couple of days.

First Work Assignments

Introduce the new employee to his trainer last. It's the old buddy system. Every new employee needs a buddy to get him started on the job and through the jungle of the first few days. The trainer should be a senior member of the team, a knowledgeable employee with good people skills.

Don't give him a tough task on the first day. Start with simple assignments well within his capacity. Your goal is to build self-confidence and a positive attitude.

The work should be useful and productive so he has a sense of accomplishment and it should pave the way for more difficult assignments later on.

If You Have Done a Good Job

- The new employee will feel part of the team from the beginning.
- He will feel he is making significant contributions to the group and the company.
- He will have confidence in you and in the company.
- He will understand the rules and their reasons.
- He won't be afraid to ask questions or appear stupid.
- He will have a positive attitude and feel good about coming to work.
- He will be motivated to learn more and move up in the company.

CHAPTER 10.

Employee Evaluations

Performance appraisal is another word for feedback—telling people how they are doing, what their strengths are and where they need to improve. If employees are not given this feedback their growth is stunted.

The formal written review probably takes place once a year, but a good manager is making appraisals, counseling, and giving feedback on a continuing basis.

The Benefits of Reviews

- Employees are more motivated. It lets them know you care about how they perform.
- It gives positive feedback to employees. Why try to do a good job if no one ever recognizes it?
- Employees learn and grow. If the employee never learns what he is doing right and what he is doing wrong he has no way of knowing that he should do things differently.
- It helps the manager plan. It gives him information about the capabilities of his team.
- It helps the company. Company-wide objectives are an accumulation of smaller ones. If employees don't meet their objectives, managers can't meet theirs, and so on up the line.
- It opens communication lines. A successful company depends on good relationships between managers and employees and good relationships depend on free and frequent communication.

Why Managers Avoid Reviews

Managers often dislike the review process. It takes time and consideration. A manager can't go into an employee review unprepared or he'll get creamed. The manager who never has the time to prepare is like the manager who never trains his people. He guarantees he never *will* have the time.

Further, a review may make a manager feel like the heavy. He may be forced to confront the employee, which could open the door to argument.

Note that if a manager doesn't correct an employee, the employee has to assume either that the manager doesn't care or that the employee is doing a good job.

In neither case does the employee have a reason to change; meanwhile, the manager gets more and more annoyed and eventually blows his stack—to the amazement of the employee.

A Review Is Good for the Company

It may be difficult and time consuming, but the benefits are many.

- It gives the employee information he needs to grow with the company.
- It gives the employee the opportunity to be heard.
- It tells an employee where he stands in the manager's, hence the company's, eyes.
- It provides written documentation of the employee's accomplishments and contributions to the company.

The Review Is Good for the Employee

It is just as difficult for the employee, but it meets some critical needs.

- It has the psychological virtue of praising improvement, no matter how small. Recognition encourages and motivates employees.
- It provides a mechanism for rewarding performance in the most important place—the pocketbook.
- It recognizes the employee's contributions and reinforces his importance to the team.

The Need for Standards

The company should provide objective standards against which to measure performance. The employee as well as the manager should be familiar with these standards.

When performance is strictly quantitative this works fine.

When performance is qualitative the good manager has to work hard at being as objective as possible. He must not be influenced by whether he likes or dislikes the person.

Consistently superior performance may indicate a lack of challenge. If the employee gets too good at the job it means he is ready for the next step—either higher standards for the same job or, better yet, a new job.

Counseling Sessions

The counseling session is an opportunity for the manager to guide employees toward improved performance. Some managers think of counseling strictly as criticism, but counseling should tell the employee:

- how well he is doing compared to company or team standards
- overall strengths and weaknesses
- opportunities for growth beyond the present job

Review Documentation

While the formal performance review may take place only once a year, the review should summarize all the shorter counseling sessions—the criticisms and the praises that were shared during the year.

Obviously, the good manager should make notes of all counseling sessions. This way, when the manager writes the review he has all the facts and information at his fingertips.

Good documentation also has important legal value in the event of a grievance claim against the company.

Review Preparation

Here is how to prepare yourself for the review:

- Allow plenty of time. You don't want yourself or the employee to be hurried.
- Schedule it when you are energetic and enthusiastic. Don't do a review when you are tired, irritable, or sick.
- Choose a place that is private and reasonably comfortable. This is a personal and confidential matter that should be treated with respect. Allow as few interruptions as possible.
- Give the employee plenty of notice and a fixed date and time. He needs to prepare as much as you do.
- Have your notes, previous reviews, job description, standards, ready at hand.
- Plan your approach.

Conducting the Review

- Remember, the employee is going to be scared. This means he may be timid and reticent or he may even be belligerent.
- Explain the purpose of the review—it is an evaluation of the employee's performance for the entire year. If you have been doing your job of counseling on a regular basis, there should be no surprises for the employee.
- Review the job description and standards so you both agree as to the basis upon which the review is being made.
- Accentuate the positive. Remember the sandwich technique—stuff a criticism between two compliments. An employee can only hear one or two negatives before an emotional door closes and nothing else gets through.
- Criticize the performance, not the person. A review should be approached as a cooperative effort. <u>The manager and the employee are equals working together to see what they can do to improve performance.</u>
- End on a positive note with a plan of action and a timetable. This enumerates what the employee can do to correct the problem, if any, sets new goals, and indicates what the manager can do to help.

The Written Report

If a complete file of notes has been accumulated during the year, the year-end report and interview should be relatively easy.

- The review should be based on the job description and standards that were explained to the employee at the beginning of the review period and again at the beginning of the review interview.
- Give specific examples of behavior and performance that support your comments. You can draw these from your notes made during the year.
- Be sure to mention accomplishments and strengths as well as weaknesses— again with specific examples. These tell the employee you were watching and he was appreciated.
- Give the employee at least a day to read the report, think about it, and come back to you with comments. This, more than anything, tells you how the employee perceived what you had said and written.

The Test of a Good Review

Can you answer yes to the following questions?

- Did the review raise the employee's morale, if at all possible?
- Did the employee leave with a clear understanding of his strengths and weaknesses?
- Did the employee have clear goals for the coming year?

CONCLUSION

The ideas expressed in this book are simple common-sense truths about people. There is nothing difficult or complicated about them. The difficulty comes in disciplining ourselves to apply these ideas on a consistent basis. We may know the correct things to do, but if we fail to do them our knowledge is wasted.

Today the business world is in desperate need of managers who are willing to take risks. It needs managers who are willing to risk using common sense and humanity, the ideas we've expressed here, as a basis for decision making.

Nothing affects employees' desire and ability to do the job more than the competence of the people who manage them. And that applies all the way up the line. What is needed in the workplace is not more sophisticated theories and models of management but a greater sensitivity to people.

While the concepts outlined in this book may seem simple, almost elementary, they are literally packed with power. Within these ideas are forgotten gems of wisdom that have the potential to revolutionize the way people manage, and consequently, to revolutionize the entire workplace.

On a more personal level, if you apply these ideas consistently you can literally change your life as a manager, provided you have the capacity to see the genius in simplicity. Some who will read this book will not at first be able to recognize these ideas as the solutions to their problems as a manager. Our complex society has taught us to be suspicious of the simple and impressed by that which we don't understand.

In this book we have presented no new facts and information on the subject of management. We have merely tried to rekindle the flame of common sense that exists in each of us. We have provided you with a guide, a mentor, if you will, for helping you use the knowledge and understanding that is already yours.

If you are a new manager we encourage you to keep your "mentor" with you at all times. We suggest that you read it over and over again until the ideas become second nature. In your first weeks and months as a manager you will probably be overwhelmed by the enormity of the task before you. This book can help you maintain your focus and sense of perspective when the world around you seems to be falling apart.

If you are an experienced manager, we suggest that you use *The First Book of Common-Sense Management* as a mirror—as a tool for taking a personal inventory of the way you manage. You may find that you are applying most of the ideas but the ideas you are not applying may be keeping you from the greater success you should be enjoying. By reading this book from time to time you can fine-tune your management practices so that you are constantly improving your effectiveness as a manager.

Regardless of how much experience you have, we invite you to become a part of the commonsense revolution. By disciplining yourself to apply these ideas on a day-to-day basis you will be doing the single most important thing you can do to ensure your own success as a manager. If managers across the country were to use these ideas as the standard for effective management, there would surely be a much-needed revolution in corporate America. We hope you will help to lead the way.

For information on management seminars and consulting services provided by Ms. Tracy,

write to:

Tracy Communications
85 Main Street, Suite 303
Hackensack, N.J. 07601